It's NOT MENOPAUSE.
I'm just like this.

Maxine's Guide to Aging Disgracefully

Illustrations by

JWagner

designed by
Barbara LaRue King

BOK2033

It's Not Menopause. I'm Just Like This.
   Maxine's Guide to Aging Disgracefully
   A Crabby Road Book

Copyright © 2003
Hallmark Licensing, Inc.

Published by Hallmark Books, a division of Hallmark Cards, Inc.,
Kansas City, MO 64141

Visit us on the web at www.Hallmark.com

Illustrations by John Wagner
Editorial Direction: Mary Gentry and Todd Hafer
Editorial Development: Jane-Elyse Pryor
   with Meghan Miller and Dave Rebeck
Art Direction: Mark Cordes
Design by Barbara LaRue King
Introductions by Dan Taylor
Maxine writers: Richard Bagley, Bill Bridgeman, Oliver Christianson,
Amie Doyen, Renee Duvall, Russ Ediger, Scott Emmons, Steve Finken,
Bill Gray, Allyson Jones, Kevin Kinzer, Mark Oatman, John Peterson,
Dee Ann Stewart, Dan Taylor, Molly Wigand, Myra Zirkle

PRINTED IN CHINA

Is it Old in Here — Or is it Just Me?

Books, magazines, movies, entire television networks, and countless "experts" are dedicated to telling us that getting old is good. Let me tell you something. In fact, I'm going to tell you whether you let me or not: *Experts who say getting old is good are not actually old.* (I wrote that slanty to make my point.)

When you're in the flabby belly of the aging beast, *that's* when you're an expert. (Again, I emphasize with slanting.)

A book about aging written by someone who's aged won't sound like other books. It'll know to speak up, and s-l-o-w-l-y.

A book about aging doesn't work unless it's written by someone who's been there and forgotten most of that.

A good aging book will make you laugh until you cough something up. It will mock. It will make fun. It will sound a little mean if you're too touchy. And if it doesn't sound a little mean, you probably aren't getting it. Where to find such a book? The same place you find gnarled knuckles and tree-root veins. That's right, in your own two hands. Grab your magnifying glass and start reading.

I've reached an age where anyone younger than me is officially a punk.

If I've said it once,
I've said it a hundred times...

(At my age, that's true of everything you can possibly ever say.)

Aging like a fine wine means spending a lot of time on your side, lying down.

Don't despair! Women are breaking down age barriers every day! Some supermodels are still successful into their late teens!

GOOD THINGS ABOUT GETTING OLDER:

Wearing bifocals says "I'm smart, I can read!"

Wrinkles around the eyes make you look happy.

Chin hairs give you something to stroke while looking thoughtful.

Gray hair is a neutral color that goes with everything.

Body Language? At My Age, It's Obscene!

There's a lot of talk these days about body image. Let me tell you something. In fact, I'm going to tell you whether you let me or not: *I have no desire to carry around an image of my body in my head.* Like a car wreck on the expressway, I understand that something unpleasant has happened and it's best not to look.

There has been a shifting and a sliding and a general re-zoning of the real estate. Believe me, the market value has plummeted. What used to be a "fixer-upper" is now the big, bad, backside of town.

No 30-day trial at any gym will sleek up the slack. No piece of equipment, no matter how easy the payments or how firm the washed-up actress touting it, will gentrify the jiggle. "Watch the carbs!" they say. "Watch the grams!" they say. "Watch your butt," I say, because I've had about enough of the idea that size matters.

I've worked out (no pun intended) a solution. I've decided not to think about my body. And like my thighs and vinyl on a muggy day, I'm sticking to that decision. As far as I'm concerned, the elastic waistband eliminated the need for scales altogether. And speaking of the altogether, when I'm in it, there are no diet experts allowed.

Know how to prevent sagging? Just eat till the wrinkles fill out.

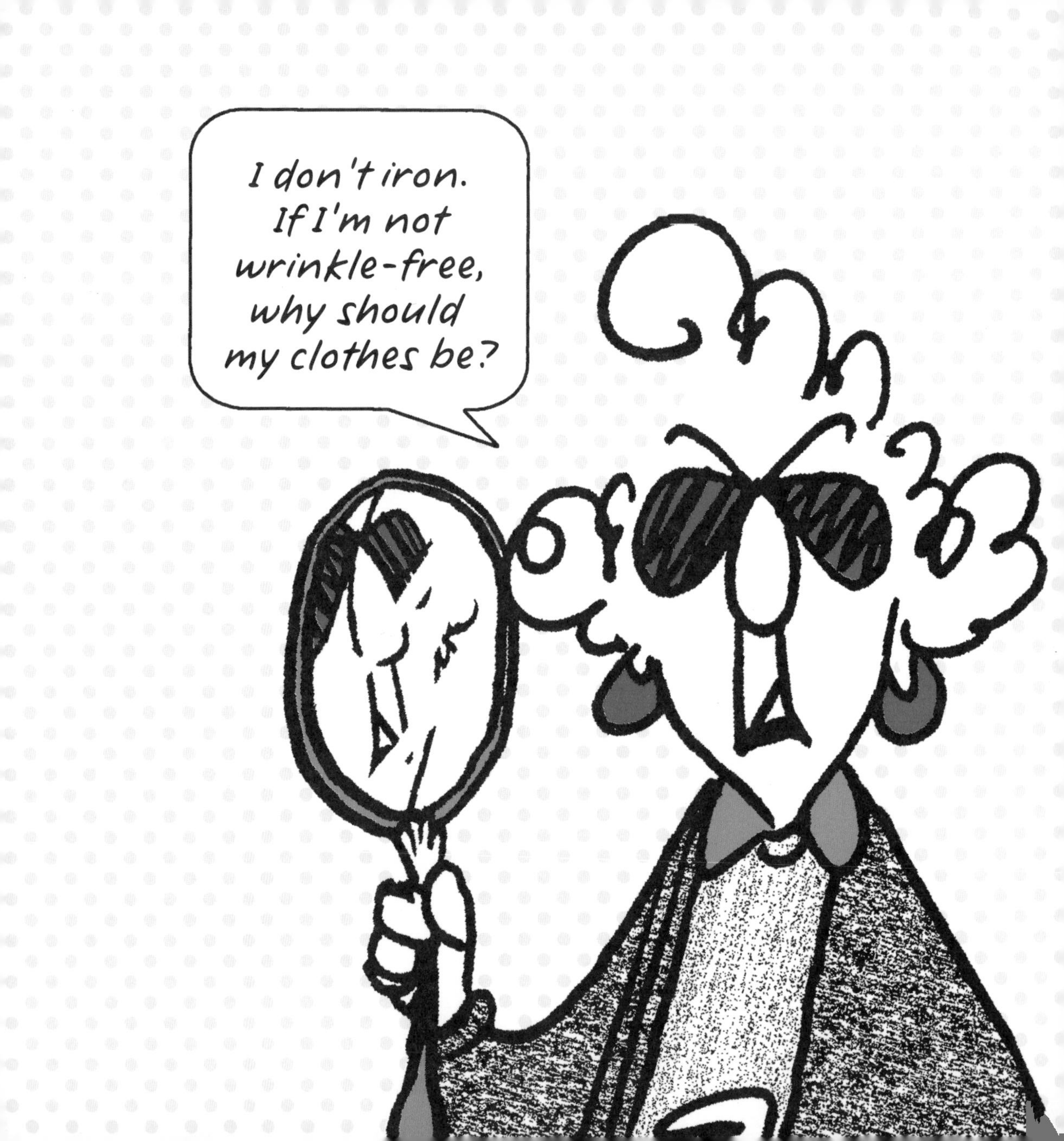
I don't iron. If I'm not wrinkle-free, why should my clothes be?

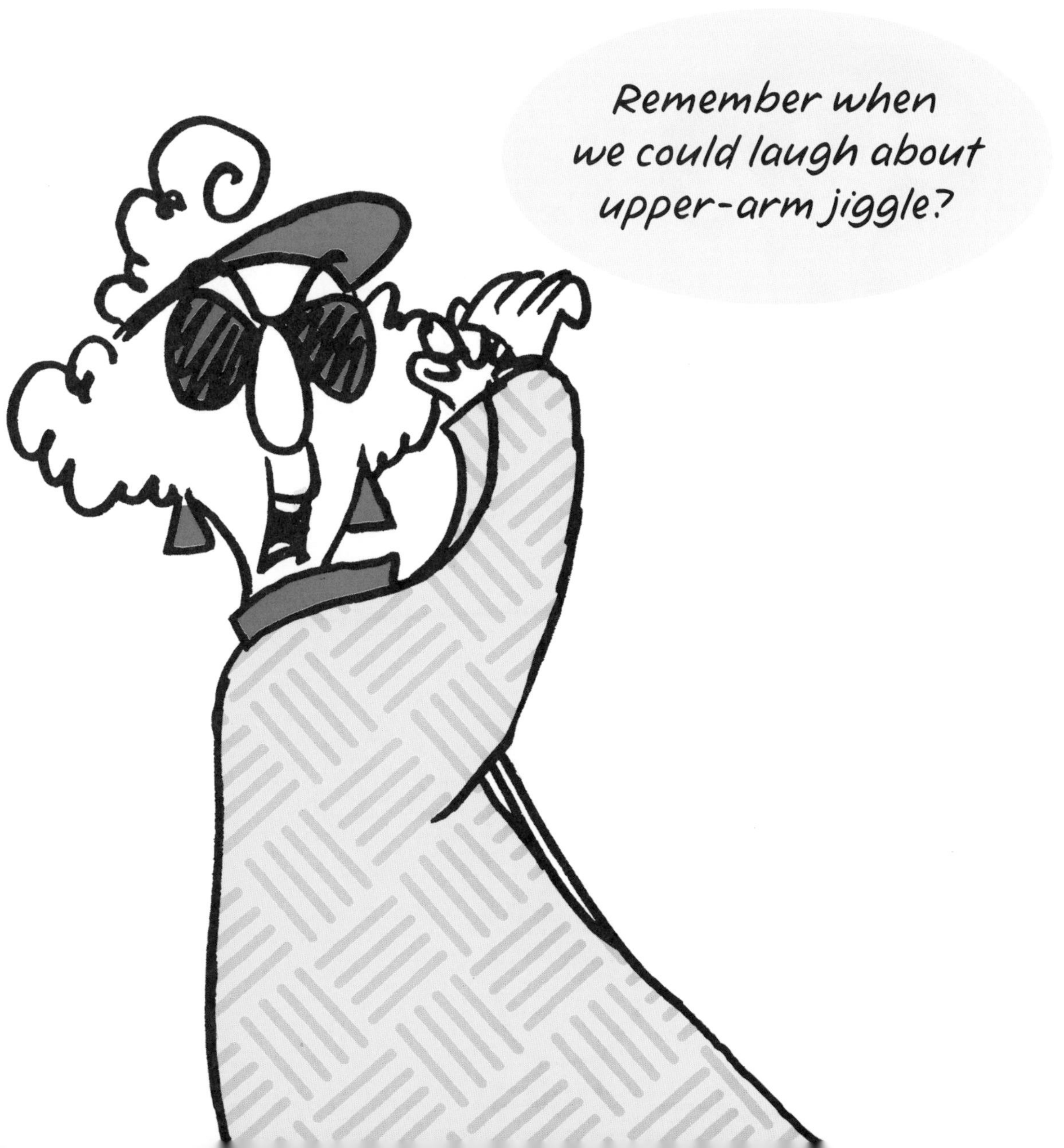
Remember when
we could laugh about
upper-arm jiggle?

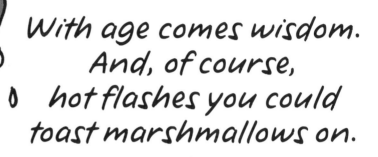

We may be older, but we're still "wonders of nature."

Yeah, we wonder what the hell nature's doing to us!

We still have the same figures we had years ago- Adjusted for inflation, of course!

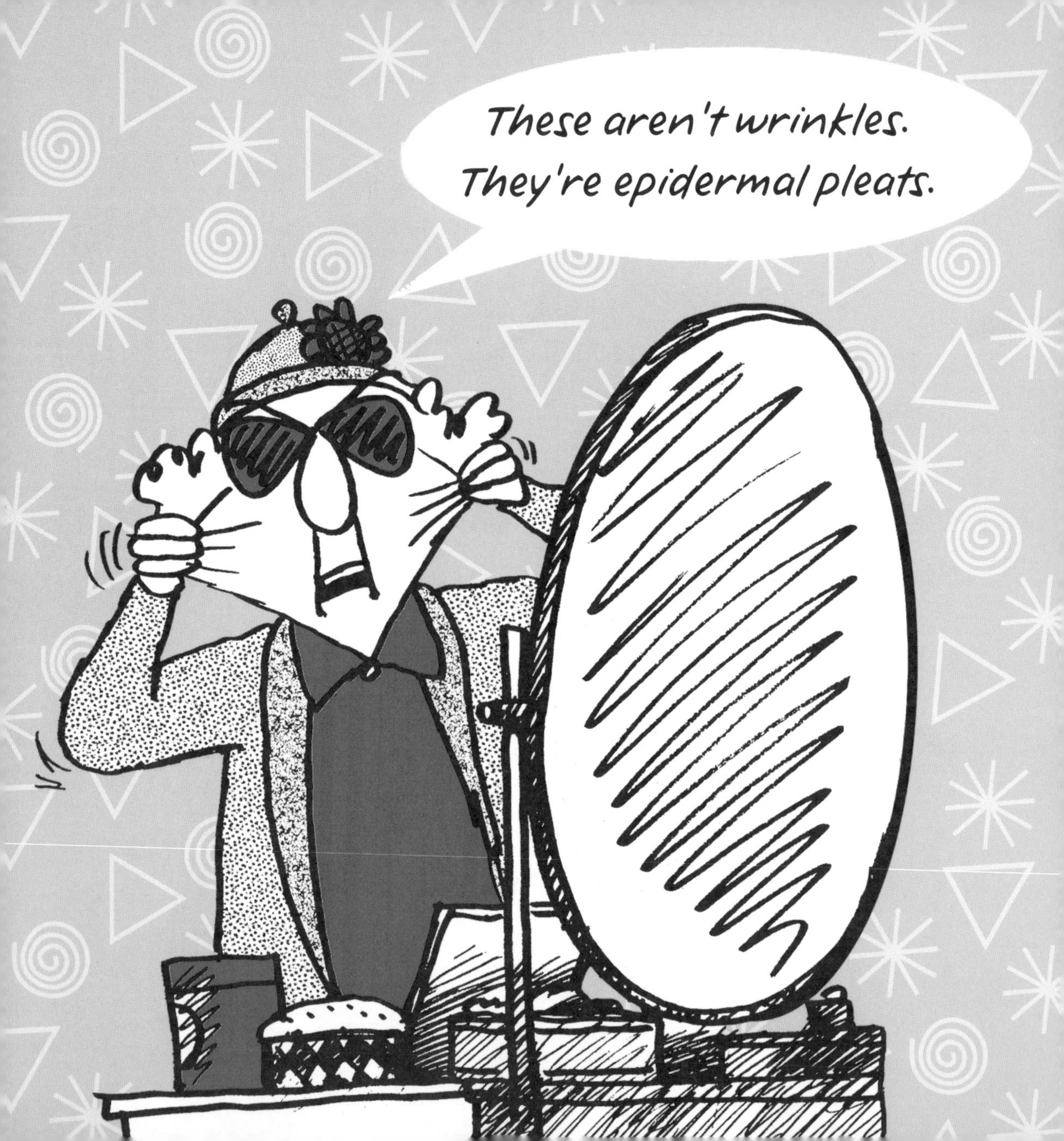
These aren't wrinkles.
They're epidermal pleats.

People our age can still enjoy an active, passionate and fulfilling sex life!
Provided we get cable. Or that dish thing.

I don't think Mother Nature is very good at Feng Shui. Just look at how she rearranged our body parts.

I can still wear a two-piece bathing suit, as long as one of 'em runs the full length of my body.

HOW TO LOOK FABULOUS IN A BATHING SUIT WITHOUT HAVING A GOOD BODY.

Happy Birthday and Other Oxymorons

If you've been paying attention, you should know that I'm going to tell you this whether you let me or not: *Birthdays for older adults are like my knees, tricky and potentially painful.*

Finding the perfect gift for an older candle-blower isn't so easy. You might get something "too young," like a skateboard or knobby-tire bike, like in the soda ads. This is basically a gift that says, "I hope you hurt yourself." You could also err on the side of "too old." This includes anything in the shawl family and clothing for cats.

You could send a card. This is something I know a little bit about. There are cards that make people laugh (my favorites) and cards that make them cry (also my favorites, but not necessarily in the intended way).

Of course, you could decide to throw a surprise party. But if you throw me a surprise party, don't be surprised to find you're the party being thrown. I didn't spend three Saturday afternoons at the Women's Defense Class for nothing.

Does it sound by now like there's really nothing to do but maybe give a birthday person money and slowly back away? If so, then you are paying attention.

The good news is that even as we get older, guys still look at our boobs. The bad news is they have to squat down first.

Maybe being our age isn't so bad.

And maybe cake doesn't have calories. Maybe gray hair is in. Maybe all size 5's are unhappy on the inside.

The older I get, the closer I get to thinking that those overnight wrinkle-sucking mud masks might really work!

Turning 50 is like visiting an all-you-can-eat buffet. What should be hot is cold, what should be firm is limp, and the buns are bigger than anything else on the menu.

As I get older, my clothes and my weight have something in common... I put on more and more of both.

When you reach my age, birthdays just aren't what they used to be... you know, fun.

If your friends can accurately guess your age, you need to find better friends.

At this time of life, birthdays bite. But they bite cautiously and chew for an extra long time.

What the Health?!

The health care industry is one of the fastest-growing industries in the last decade. Let me tell you something. In fact, I'm going to tell you whether you've got your miracle ear turned up or not: *"Health care" is one of those phrases where the two things don't go together.* Like "jumbo shrimp" or "comfortable futon." You know those phrases, oxy-ex-husbands or something like that.

Take menopause, for example. Hey! You can have mine, it certainly isn't doing me any good. No matter what your symptom: can't sleep, can't eat, can't get warm, can't get cold, itchy foot, someone's going to tell you it's menopause. I think the word means "Men pause while they make something up."

And if it's not that, it's diet and exercise. Diet and exercise, diet and exercise, always together, like they're joined at the artificial hip. Can't it be one or the other? Or my favorite, neither?

I would pay a doctor to leave me alone. We've worked hard for the right to wear a sweater when it's 90° in the Shady Acres. If you're hungry, eat! It won't kill you. Not eating, now that'll kill you. When it comes to your health, maybe not caring is the healthiest thing you can do.

When did
fun get to be
so much
work?

Welcome to the years when the popping of our knees is drowned out by the sound of groaning when we stand up.